D1558616

3/07

The Lost Colony of Roanoke

A Primary Source History

The Rosen Publishing Group's

PowerKids Press™

New York

Jake Miller

Published in 2006 by The Rosen Publishing Group, Inc.
29 East 21st Street, New York, NY 10010

First Edition

Editor: Jennifer Way
Book Design: Ginny Chu

Photo Credits: Cover, pp. 6, 14 (inset) © North Wind Picture Archives; pp. 4, 12 Picture Collection, The Branch Libraries, The New York Public Library, Astor, Lenox, and Tilden Foundations; pp. 4 (inset), 12 (inset) © Corbis; p. 6 (inset) Kunsthistorisches Museum, Vienna, Austria/Bridgeman Art Library; p. 8 © The Mariners' Museum/Corbis; p. 8 (inset) © Yale Center for British Art, Paul Mellon Collection, USA/Bridgeman Art Library; p. 10 © Archivo Iconografico, S.A./Corbis; pp. 10 (inset), 17 © Bettmann/Corbis; pp. 11, 14 Private Collection/Bridgeman Art Library; p. 16 Erich Lessing / Art Resource, NY; p. 16 (inset) from The Virginia Adventure, The University Press of Virginia; p. 18 The New York Public Library/Art Resource, NY; p. 18 (inset) © Getty Images; p. 20 National Park Service, Fort Raleigh National Historic Site; p. 20 (inset) Collection of East Carolina University, photo courtesy of the National Parks Service, used by permission of Charles R. Ewen, PhD.

Library of Congress Cataloging-in-Publication Data

Miller, Jake, 1969–
    The lost colony of Roanoke : a primary source history / Jake Miller. — 1st ed.
        p. cm. — (The primary source library of the thirteen colonies and the Lost Colony)
    Includes bibliographical references (p.   ) and index.
    ISBN 1-4042-3027-0 (library binding)
    1. Roanoke Colony—Juvenile literature. 2. Roanoke Island (N.C.)—History—16th century—Juvenile literature.   I. Title. II. Series.

F229.M645 2006
975.6'175—dc22

2004019476

Manufactured in the United States of America

Contents

This nineteenth-century painting imagines Philip Amadas and Arthur Barlowe's 1584 landing in Virginia. Inset: Theodor de Bry created this 1590 map of the Americas. It shows how people believed North America and South America looked. Around the map are pictures of the men who explored the Americas.

Exploring the New World

In the 1500s, European nations such as Spain and France were **exploring** the Americas. They called it the New World. These nations were looking for lands with valuable **resources**, such as gold, furs, or spices. England was a small nation that was just starting to become powerful. They wanted to find places to start a colony where no other country had one.

One of the first places in which England tried to make a colony was Roanoke Island, on the East Coast of North America. The English tried twice to start a colony there, but both attempts failed. The second settlement of Roanoke, begun in 1587, has become a famous mystery. By 1590, all the **colonists** had disappeared, and Roanoke became known as the Lost Colony.

Roanoke Island can be seen inside the yellow circle on this map of the Virginia Territory and the Chesapeake Bay. Inset: Sir Walter Raleigh received many official appointments and land grants from Elizabeth I. He is shown here in an anonymous sixteenth-century painting.

Sir Walter Raleigh

In 1584, Elizabeth I, queen of England, asked Sir Walter Raleigh to establish an English colony in North America. The sailors he sent claimed a large part of the East Coast and named it Virginia. Raleigh then sent Philip Amadas and Arthur Barlowe to an area of Virginia that is now North Carolina. They found an island that they thought would be a good place to start a colony.

Native Americans lived on the island. They were friendly to the explorers. Amadas and Barlowe named the island Roanoke Island for these people. They brought two Native Americans, named Wanchese and Manteo, back to England.

Sir Walter Raleigh

Sir Walter Raleigh was born around 1554 in England. He was a soldier who won the attention of Queen Elizabeth I, who knighted him in 1585.

Although Raleigh arranged journeys to North America, he never set foot there. Raleigh was put to death by King James I in 1618. The capital of North Carolina, Raleigh, is named for him.

This man, drawn by Theodor de Bry in the 1580s, is from the village of Pomeioc, an area nearby the Roanoke Colony. Inset: De Bry's drawings were based on those by John White. White's drawings recorded the people, plants, and animals of the Roanoke area. Some of these plants and animals, such as this brown pelican, had never before been seen by the English.

Pictures of the New World

In the spring of 1585, Sir Walter Raleigh sent 108 men to Roanoke Island. One of the leaders was Sir Richard Grenville, the captain of the ships. The other was General Ralph Lane, who would be the leader on land. Manteo also joined this journey to help the colonists talk to other Native Americans.

The men arrived at Roanoke on July 11. The first thing they did was to explore the nearby islands and the **mainland**. They saw plants and animals that no Englishman had seen before. A painter named John White made a record of these things. He painted Native American villages, animals, and plants. The group built a **fort**, which became known as Fort Raleigh. Grenville soon realized that they needed more supplies from England. On August 25, he sailed back to England. Lane remained in charge.

De Bry drew this picture of an Algonquin village around 1591. Inset: This map shows where different Native American groups lived around 1650. The Algonquin people, of which the Native Americans around Roanoke were a part, lived throughout much of Virginia and along the East Coast.

Failure of the First Colony

While the soldiers waited for Grenville to return, Lane and his men tried to force the **Algonquin** Native Americans who lived nearby to feed them. The English soldiers were used to having people follow their orders. The English burned villages and killed a leader named Secotan. This made the Algonquins angry and scared, and they refused to work with the English.

Nearly a year had gone by since Grenville had left, and he had not returned. In June 1586, an English captain named Sir Francis Drake sailed by Roanoke. All but 15 men decided to leave the colony with Drake. The first colony was a failure.

Algonquin Villages

There were more than 5,000 Algonquins living in the area around Roanoke Island when the English arrived. Some of them lived in villages and towns with names such as Aquasogoc and Secota.

The towns and farms were banded together into kingdoms. The Algonquins grew corn, squash, and tobacco. They also hunted deer and caught fish.

The painting above imagines the colonists' landing on Roanoke. Inset: The settlers who went to Roanoke in 1587 only wanted to stop on the island before moving north to the Chesapeake Bay area, which is shown on this map. They hoped the soil there would be better for farming than Roanoke's.

A Second Colony

In May 1587, Raleigh sent another group of colonists to the New World. There were about 117 settlers, including women and children. Each colonist had to pay for his or her own trip. In return for his **investment**, each man would get 500 acres (202 ha) of land and a say in the colonial government. John White was appointed **governor** of the colony.

Raleigh directed White to stop at Roanoke to check on the 15 soldiers who had been left behind two years earlier. The ship would then sail farther north to the **Chesapeake Bay** to settle. The colonists wanted to go where the Native Americans were not angry with the English. They also wanted to go where the farming would be better. Roanoke had experienced a period of dry weather, which had made the soil bad for farming.

This map shows Roanoke (circled), and the Chesapeake Bay. Early colonists had hoped that this location would protect them from attack from enemy navies. Inset: By 1587, the once-friendly relations between the settlers and the Native Americans had fallen apart and both groups feared one another.

Landing at Roanoke

The colonists sailed with a Portuguese-born captain named Simon Fernandez. He did not want to take the settlers to the Chesapeake Bay. Upon landing at Roanoke on July 22, Fernandez made the settlers get off the boat and landed nearby while they unloaded their supplies.

The settlers made a strange discovery when they reached the island. All 15 men from the first colony were gone. Manteo had gone to England with Lane and had returned to Roanoke with White's colonists. He found that his people in **Croatoan** were no longer friendly with the English. The soldiers' bullying had hurt the settlers' chances at living peacefully with the Native Americans. The colonists believed it was unsafe to stay on Roanoke and wanted to move on to the Chesapeake Bay.

White had trouble getting back to Roanoke because in 1588 England was fighting the powerful Spanish navy, shown above. England's success assured its place as a growing European power. Inset: This 1851 woodcut imagines how the Roanoke Colony may have looked when the second group of settlers lived there.

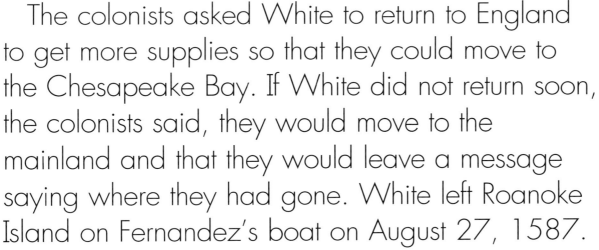

Trouble at Sea

The colonists asked White to return to England to get more supplies so that they could move to the Chesapeake Bay. If White did not return soon, the colonists said, they would move to the mainland and that they would leave a message saying where they had gone. White left Roanoke Island on Fernandez's boat on August 27, 1587.

When White got to England, the country was about to go to war with Spain. The English needed all the boats they had to fight Spain's navy. It would be nearly three years before White could find a boat that would take him back to Roanoke.

Virginia Dare

On August 18, 1587, one of the colonists, Eleanor Dare, gave birth to a girl. Her name was Virginia Dare. She was the first baby born in America with English parents. Governor John White was Eleanor's father and Virginia's grandfather.

A briefe and true report of the new found land of Virginia. of the commodities and of the nature and manners of the naturall inhabitants. Difcouered by the English Colony there feated by Sir Richard Greinuile Knight In the yeere 1585. Which Remained Vnder the gouernement of twelue monethes, At the fpeciall charge and direction of the Honourable SIR WALTER RALEIGH Knight lord Warden of the ftanneries Who therein hath beene fauoured and authorifed by her MAIESTIE and her letters patents: This fore booke Is made in English By Thomas Hariot feruant to the abouenamed Sir WALTER, a member of the Colony, and there, imployed in difcouering CVM GRATIA ET PRIVILEGIO CÆS.MA.TIS SPECIA.LI

FRANCOFORTI AD MOENVM TYPIS IOANNIS WECHELI, SVMTIBVS VERO THEODORI DE BRY ANNO CIƆ IƆ XC. VENALES REPERIVNTVR IN OFFICINA SIGISMVNDI FEIRABENDII

from A briefe and true report

"A briefe and true report of the new found land of Virginia of the commodities and of the nature and manners of the naturall inhabitants. Discovered by the English Colony there . . . in 1585."

This title page from Thomas Hariot's A brief and true report of the new found land of Virginia was originally published in 1590. This title page says that the book will describe the land, animals, and people found in Virginia. The page is decorated with pictures of Native Americans that are based on White's drawings.

When White returned to Roanoke in 1590, he found only the word "Cro" cut into a tree, and "Croatoan" cut into a post. He soon had to leave and was never able to return to the area to look for more clues. Inset: White's drawings were used in this 1590 book.

18

The Colony Is Lost

At last, on August 18, 1590, White returned to Roanoke. When he landed he saw the word "Cro" written on a tree on shore. It must have been a message from the colonists, but he did not know what it meant. He went to the village. When he got there, the settlers were all gone. Wherever they went, they had taken almost all of their belongings with them. They had even taken apart the houses and carried away the nails.

Just about the only things left were the posts of a fence they had built around their village. On one of the posts, White found the word "Croatoan." As soon as he saw the word, White wanted to go to Manteo's hometown of Croatoan on a nearby island. White knew it was a message from the colonists. He hoped he would find the colonists waiting for him there.

There have been many digs on Roanoke, but archaeologists have found few clues and no solid proof as to what happened to the Lost Colony of 1587. Inset: A treasure-hunting Civil War soldier found this ax head on Roanoke Island in the 1860s.

A Mystery

Before White could get to Croatoan to search for clues, a terrible storm blew up. The captain of the ship said in those rough waters it would be unsafe to continue to Croatoan. John White had no choice but to sail back to England. He never returned to Roanoke or to America. He never saw his daughter or his granddaughter, Virginia Dare, again.

No one knows where the Roanoke colonists went. Some historians think that the colonists were killed by Native Americans. Others think they moved to Croatoan or to the mainland. They think that perhaps the colonists learned to live with the Native Americans in peace, even marrying into each other's families. Other English colonists who came to America later searched for clues but never found any proof of what happened.

Roanoke Island Today

Roanoke Island is now part of North Carolina in the United States. The island has two towns, a fishing village named Wanchese and a beach **resort** called Manteo. There is also a national historic area called Fort Raleigh with a **re-creation** of Ralph Lane's fort. **Archaeologists** are not sure if the historic area is the exact location of the Lost Colony.

No one has ever found the remains of the houses or the post where the colonists left their message. The coastlines of North Carolina and Roanoke have moved over the years, so the place where the buildings were may now be underwater. After 400 years, the clues are harder than ever to find, but historians and archaeologists still hope to solve the mystery of the Lost Colony.

Glossary

Algonquin (al-GAHN-kwin) Native Americans who lived in eastern North America.

archaeologists (ar-kee-AH-luh-jists) People who study the remains of peoples to understand how they lived.

Chesapeake Bay (CHEH-suh-peek BAY) Part of the Atlantic Ocean located between Maryland and Virginia.

colonists (KAH-luh-nists) People who live in a colony.

Croatoan (kroh-uh-TOH-in) Name of the people and of a town on an island near Roanoke.

exploring (ek-SPLOR-ing) Traveling and looking for new land.

fort (FORT) A strong building or place that can be defended against an enemy.

governor (GUH-vuh-nur) An official that is put in charge of a colony by a king or a queen.

investment (in-VEST-ment) Putting money into something, such as a company, in the hope of getting more money later on.

mainland (MAYN-lund) The main part of the land. Not an island.

re-creation (ree-kree-AY-shun) Something that has been built to look like something from the past.

resort (rih-ZORT) A vacation spot, which usually includes a hotel.

resources (REE-sors-ez) Supplies or sources of energy or useful items.

Index

Primary Sources

Page 4. Inset. *Map of the Americas With Portraits of Christopher Columbus, Amerigo Vespucci, Ferdinand Magellan, and Francisco Pizarro.* 1590, Theodor de Bry. **Page 6.** *The Arrival of the English in Virginia, from 'Admiranda Narratio.'* Colored engraving, circa sixteenth century, Theodor de Bry, Service Historique de la Marine, Vincennes, France. **Inset.** *Sir Walter Raleigh.* Painting, circa sixteenth century, Kunsthistorisches Museum, Vienna, Austria. **Page 8.** *An Aged Man in His Winter Garment.* Hand-colored engraving after drawing by John White 1590, Theodor de Bry, The Mariners' Museum. **Inset.** *Head of a Brown Pelican, after the original by John White.* Pencil and watercolor, nineteenth-century reproduction of 1584 original, P.D.H. Page, Yale Center for British Art, Paul Mellon Collection. **Page 10.** *The Town of Pomeioc.* Hand-colored engraving after drawing by John White circa 1591, Theodor de Bry. **Page 11.** *The Village of Secoton.* Hand-colored engraving after drawing by John White circa 1590s, Theodor de Bry, Service Historique de la Marine, Vincennes, France. **Page 12. Inset.** *Chesapeake Bay and the Potomac River, labeled in Latin,* 1671. **Page 14.** *Map of Raleigh's Virginia.* Lithograph, 16th century, John White, private collection. **Page 16.** *Sea battle between the Spanish Armada and English naval forces.* Oil-on-canvas, circa 1600, Hendrik Cornelisz Vroom. **Page 18. Inset.** *A briefe and true report of the new found land of Virginia.* 1588, Thomas Hariot.

Web Sites

Due to the changing nature of Internet links, PowerKids Press has developed an online list of Web sites related to the subject of this book. This site is updated regularly. Please use this link to access the list:
www.powerkidslinks.com/pstclc/roanoke/